I was one of the millions of young people inspired by Ronald Reagan's election in 1980. I was thirteen years old and remember vividly the campaign and election night. I later worked on his reelection as a teenage Republican and on his legislative agenda as an aide at the U.S. Senate Steering Committee. I spent my four years of high school and four years of college during his two terms in office. Much of that time was spent defending President Reagan and his agenda to my teachers, college professors, and classmates.

In May of 1991 I travelled to Los Angeles for a private meeting with the former president. It was a rain check for a photo that I was supposed to have taken with him while he was in the White House. He greeted me with a disarming assertion: "I've been waiting for this picture for some time." He was

Ronald Wilson Reagan

special, but he made me feel special. He made me feel comfortable with his kind, deep blue eyes and warm smile. I was in the presence of greatness, but he was a most humble hero.

I wrote this biography with the help of the more than twenty-five books I have read about President Reagan, interviews with those touched by President Reagan, and my own personal experiences watching this great American. Little original material is presented here and I have listed my primary sources of research in the bibliography at the end of this book. All indented quotes in this book are direct quotes from Ronald Reagan. I have attempted to collect and write about the human being behind the man who served magnificently as leader of the free world. Ronald Wilson Reagan was extraordinary, but he also suffered and struggled and felt heartbreak and disappointment along the way to greatness. I hope this book will be an inspiration to young readers and a fond reminder to those who remember when he was president.

Greg Rothman

Life-Changing Classics, Volume XII

Ronald Wilson Reagan
The Great Communicator

Greg Rothman

Life-Changing Classics, Volume XII

**Ronald Wilson Reagan:
The Great Communicator**

Published by
Tremendous Life Books
206 West Allen Street
Mechanicsburg, PA 17055
717-766-9499   800-233-2665
Fax: 717-766-6565
www.TremendousLifeBooks.com

Copyright © 2011 Tremendous Life Books
All rights reserved.

ISBN: 978-1-936354-10-8

Printed in the United States of America

TABLE OF CONTENTS

Introduction 5

Ronald Wilson Reagan:
The Great Communicator 7

Bibliography 35

About the Author 37

RONALD WILSON REAGAN:
The Great Communicator

Ronald Reagan was one of the most popular presidents in our nation's history. His efforts not only led to peace and prosperity, but he also restored pride in America and exported freedom and democracy around the world. During his presidency, Reagan often spoke of America as a "shining city on the hill"—a biblical reference. His unbridled optimism and unwavering belief in American ideals led the nation out of economic malaise and into the greatest peacetime economic expansion in history. He believed in the American Dream because his life was proof of its existence.

Reagan also believed in American exceptionalism, calling the United States the "last, great hope for freedom." Reagan believed that the American people could accomplish

Ronald Wilson Reagan

great things because of the liberty and freedom they were granted. His desk had a red leather frame with his message in gold letters: "It CAN Be Done." His story is an American story, complete with struggle, optimism, hope, heartbreak, perseverance, sacrifice, triumph, and greatness.

> Whatever else history may say about me when I'm gone, I hope it will record that I appealed to your best hopes, not your worst fears; to your confidence rather than your doubts. My dream is that you will travel the road ahead with liberty's lamp guiding your steps and opportunity's arm steadying your way.

Ronald Wilson Reagan was born on February 6, 1911, in Tampico, Illinois. As a young adult, he lived through the "cheerless and desperate days" of the Great Depression. John Edward "Jack" Reagan, his father, was a proud Irish Catholic who dressed to impress and drank to excess. As Jack Reagan's abuse of alcohol got worse, his loving wife Nelle would demonstrate her unconditional love by praying for him continually.

The Great Communicator

> My mother would pray constantly for him. She was on her knees several times a day. And she just refused to give up, no matter how dark things looked.

From his mother, young Ronald would learn to be optimistic and hopeful and know the value of prayer. From his father, he would learn hard work and style and perhaps some humility. In his autobiography, Reagan tells the story of finding his father passed out in the front yard in the snow. The eleven-year-old son considered walking past his father, but instead carried him into the house. Ronald must have also learned forgiveness as Jack Reagan's son. Ronald would also say he learned ambition from his father and "maybe a little something about telling a story."

"Dutch," as Ronald Reagan would become known, learned to have faith in God from his mother. He would say, "Within the covers of the Bible are all the answers for all the problems men face." He was raised in Dixon, Illinois, in a modest home. From both of his parents he learned about tolerance and loyalty. His parents remained married through

Ronald Wilson Reagan

poverty, numerous moves, and the private and public humiliation due to Jack Reagan's troubles with alcohol. Ronald and his older brother Neil would observe that the love between their mother and father could not be broken. According to his mother, forgiveness was a primary Christian tenet. President Reagan would demonstrate the ultimate personification of forgiveness when he requested prayers for John Hinckley Jr., the man who shot him in an assassination attempt.

Reagan believed that God had blessed America and that Americans had a special relationship with their Creator. Reagan's daughter Patti said about her father, "He did have something special with God; he talked to God all the time. . . . He just had conversations with God."

One day when he was thirteen or fourteen, his father took the family on a Sunday afternoon drive in the country. Young Reagan picked up his mother's glasses that she had left in the backseat and put them on. He let out a yell that alarmed the passengers and driver of the car. He had never seen cows,

The Great Communicator

words on billboards, or leaves on the trees. He said later, "I'd discovered a world I didn't know existed before." He sat in the front row of class and just assumed he could see only what everyone else saw. Suddenly, the reason that he was not able to hit a baseball became clearer. It turned out that he was horribly nearsighted, and after getting glasses he became a better athlete.

Before graduating from high school, he added three inches to get to his near six-foot frame and was elected president of the Dixon High School Student Council. He also participated in debates and ran track. He was a legendary lifeguard at the Lowell Park Lake, rescuing a total of seventy-seven people in seven summers. Reagan reveled in his role as lifeguard.

After finishing high school, Dutch went to Eureka College where he played football and acted in school plays. He struggled to find a job after graduating from college in 1932 and would travel on unsuccessful job hunting trips. His father told him about a sports department manager job at a new Montgomery Ward set

Ronald Wilson Reagan

to open in town. He interviewed for the job and set his heart on it. If he had landed that job, we may have only known about Ronald Reagan as president of Montgomery Ward.

> I was raised to believe that God has a plan for everyone and that seemingly random twists of fate are all a part of His plan.

The job went to a classmate who was a better athlete.

Instead, his first job out of college was as a sparsely paid sports announcer for WOC Radio in Davenport, Iowa, in 1933. One of his responsibilities was announcing the Chicago Cubs baseball games. On this job he learned to speak to the heartland of America as he painted pictures with his words. In 1935 Ron Reagan enlisted in the Army Reserves and served in the Army Air Corps. He went to Los Angeles for the Cubs spring training and through a twist of fate ended up meeting with an agent who got him a screen test.

In April 1937 Warner Brothers gave him a seven-year contract. He would appear in fifty-four feature films over the next quarter

The Great Communicator

of a century. In Hollywood he learned to act and play a role, but he also learned humility that would allow him to delegate important responsibilities to aides or to allow others to get the credit. "It is amazing what can be accomplished if you don't mind who gets the credit," he said often.

His time in Hollywood would be marked with a continuing struggle for recognition, success, and ultimately, some would say, relevance. He was typecast as the loyal friend to the star, the second fiddle, the bridesmaid. For the actor Ronald Reagan, 1941 would be his best year in pictures. He starred in his two most acclaimed films, *Knute Rockne: All American* and *Santa Fe Trail*.

An acting career did not give Reagan the purpose in life he was searching for; instead he found it in politics. His first encounter with politics was during his term as president of the Screen Actors Guild, during the crisis over the infiltration of Hollywood by radical communists and foreign influence. He feared Hollywood was moving from a place where American heroes and American ideals were

Ronald Wilson Reagan

celebrated to a leftist propaganda machine that no longer respected the values that made our country great.

On January 26, 1940, at age twenty-nine, he married Hollywood actress Jane Wyman. They would be married for nine years. While his wife's career soared, his was stagnant. Wyman would win an Academy Award for best actress and have a public affair that would break Ronald Reagan's heart. A week after his thirty-eighth birthday, Wyman filed for divorce, and Reagan couldn't even bear to attend the hearing. Wyman sought and received full-time custody of the children: Maureen was seven years old, and Michael was three. Reagan would get weekend visitation rights. He was shocked and sad. He was also full of shame, feeling as if he had failed publicly at the most important thing in his life. It was reported that he did a lot of crying on a lot of shoulders. That openly heartbroken time may have influenced the more emotionally detached man who would become president.

In November 1949 Ronald Reagan re-

The Great Communicator

ceived a phone call from a twenty-eight-year-old actress named Nancy Davis, who was asking the Screen Actors Guild president to do her a political favor. She later admitted that she was just looking for an excuse to call him because she was interested in meeting him. He also later admitted that he did her the favor because he wanted to meet her.

Nancy was from Chicago, the stepdaughter of a prominent neurosurgeon named Loyal Davis. She was new to Hollywood, but had dated several Hollywood stars including Clark Gable. The Hollywood tabloids took notice of Ronald and Nancy's courtship, and one gossip columnist referred to it as a "romance of a couple who have no vices."

After three years of dating, Reagan proposed to Nancy. They married in a private and quiet ceremony on March 5, 1952. Reagan would say, "Nancy saved my life." They had two children together: Patti Davis and Ronald Reagan Jr. For the next half century, Nancy was Ronald Reagan's best friend, confidante, soul mate, and promoter. She also protected her beloved Ronnie, and

Ronald Wilson Reagan

theirs would be a genuine and lasting love affair.

From 1954 to 1962 Ronald Reagan became a regular on the chicken-dinner circuit, traveling the country giving speeches for General Electric as an "Ambassador of Goodwill." During these dinner talks to civic groups throughout the country, Reagan would listen to the aspirations of the American people and would also express his message of American optimism as it related to the American Dream. He served as host of a popular Sunday evening television program called *General Electric Theater*. In eight years he visited 139 GE research and manufacturing facilities and met with over 250,000 individual employees of GE.

His honed stump speech was one of optimism, hope, and opportunity for America. He would say,

> There are no such things as limits to growth, because there are no limits to the human capacity for intelligence, imagination, and wonder.

The Great Communicator

In 1964 Ronald Reagan—the former self-described "FDR Democrat"—gave a critical nationally televised speech titled "A Time for Choosing" on behalf of Republican presidential candidate Arizona Senator Barry Goldwater. The "Time for Choosing" speech that later became known as "the Goldwater speech" was filled with themes that Reagan would champion for the next quarter century.

> And this idea that government is beholden to the people, that it has no other source of power except the sovereign people, is still the newest and most unique idea in all the long history of man's relation to man. This is the issue of this election. Whether we believe in our capacity for self-government or whether we abandon the American Revolution and confess that a little intellectual elite in a far-distant capital can plan our lives for us better than we can plan for ourselves.

Goldwater lost badly to President Lyndon Johnson, who was running for reelection, but Reagan emerged as the new favorite of the

Ronald Wilson Reagan

conservative movement. Reagan would also become the heir apparent to Goldwater.

The Goldwater speech, the SAG presidency, and the experience on the chicken-dinner circuit with General Electric—along with some urging from wife Nancy and from some prominent California businesspeople—led Reagan to run for and be elected as governor of California in 1966.

Some have said that Ronald Reagan was an ordinary man who did extraordinary things and that he was a reluctant leader. Perhaps the notion that he was a former actor who was not even a Hollywood leading man caused some to assume that he was not a bona fide leader. On the contrary, he was an outspoken student leader in high school and college. As a leader of the Screen Actors Guild, he was also a man who knew what he believed and was willing to say it out loud. <u>Ronald Reagan believed in leadership by delegating and inspiring.</u>

> The greatest leader is not necessarily the one who does the greatest things. He is the one that gets the people to do the greatest things.

The Great Communicator

He realized that the people, not government, did great things.

In 1968 Reagan ran for the Republican nomination for president. The Republican primary that year would feature numerous candidates challenging the front-runner, former vice president Richard Nixon. Aided by a huge win in the California primary where his name was the only Republican one on the ballot, Reagan actually won the popular vote nationally, 1,696,632 (37.93 percent) to Nixon's 1,679,443 (37.54 percent), but lost the nomination because he finished third in the battle for delegates.

In 1970 Reagan was reelected governor of California with nearly 53 percent of the vote. The 1970s was a time of unrest and cynicism in the United States. The Vietnam War, Watergate, the oil crisis, inflation, excesses of the hippies, and corruption in government would create an electorate that was angry and upset, demanding more accountability in government. In 1976 the Democrats would choose Jimmy Carter as their nominee—a peanut farmer and former governor of Georgia, who

Ronald Wilson Reagan

had a master's degree in nuclear physics and a background working in the navy's nuclear submarine program.

The GOP convention in 1976 would be the second presidential heartbreak for Ronald Reagan. For his allies in the conservative movement, it would be the third straight disappointment, starting with Barry Goldwater in 1964.

In 1976, upset with President Gerald Ford's capitulation in dealing with the Soviets, Reagan challenged a sitting incumbent president from within the party and nearly won the Republican nomination. Gerald Ford had replaced Nixon, who resigned after the Watergate scandal. Few people remember that Reagan suffered a heartbreaking loss in 1976. He battled during the primaries and lost a convention-floor fight as Ford received 1,187 delegates to Reagan's 1,070 delegates. No Republican nominating convention has been that close since.

The next day Reagan gave a speech to his supporters.

The Great Communicator

> The cause goes on. It's just one battle in a long war, and it will go on as long as we all live. . . . Don't give up your ideals. Don't compromise. Don't turn to expediency. And don't for heaven's sake, having seen the inner workings of the watch, don't get cynical. . . . Recognize that there are millions and millions of Americans out there who want what you want. Who want it to be that way—who want it to be a shining city on a hill . . .

Reagan campaigned in twenty states for Ford, but Ford was narrowly defeated by Jimmy Carter and his vice presidential running mate Senator Walter Mondale. The day after Jimmy Carter won the 1976 presidential election, Ronald Reagan and his team would begin their third presidential campaign, which would ultimately lead to a victory that would promote him to the Oval Office in 1981.

In terms of public opinion, many people view Jimmy Carter as the worst president in modern history from the standpoint of both domestic and foreign policy. America would face a malaise at home and shrinking respect abroad. Tax rates and spending soared as a

Ronald Wilson Reagan

post-Watergate Democratic Party controlled both the House of Representatives and the U.S. Senate.

Carter's economic policies of tax and spend led the country into a recession. America was faced with a "misery index," high inflation, high unemployment, high interest rates, high taxes, and low morale. Reagan would quip,

> A recession is when your neighbor loses his job. A depression is when you lose your job. A recovery is when Jimmy Carter loses his job.

Foreign policy also suffered under the Carter-Mondale administration. The Soviet Union expanded in Afghanistan and exported Communism to Africa and Central and Latin America. On November 4, 1979, an angry mob of young Islamic revolutionaries overran the U.S. Embassy in Tehran, taking sixty-six Americans hostage. During the final year of Carter's tenure as the nation's chief executive, the hostages remained captive, and Carter's inability to deal successfully

The Great Communicator

with the hostage crisis and other problems at home and abroad led to an overwhelming defeat in his bid for reelection. Sixty-nine-year-old Ronald Reagan was elected America's fortieth president on November 4, 1980, in a landslide victory over the incumbent. On January 20, 1981, the hostages were released moments after Reagan and Vice President George H. W. Bush were inaugurated.

On March 30, 1981, John Hinckley Jr. attempted to assassinate the president at the Washington Hilton Hotel. Reagan was shot but maintained his legendary sense of humor: When one of the doctors informed President Ronald Reagan that they were going to operate on him, the president said, "I hope you're a Republican." The doctor looked at President Reagan and said, "Today, Mr. President, we're all Republicans." When his wife Nancy arrived at the hospital he said to her, "Honey, I forgot to duck," borrowing Jack Dempsey's line to his wife the night he was beaten by Gene Tunney for the heavyweight championship. Reagan believed that he was spared by Providence for a special purpose. Within two

Ronald Wilson Reagan

weeks, Pope John Paul II also survived an assassination attempt. Subsequently, President Reagan and the pope along with British Prime Minister Margaret Thatcher would share in a desire to bring freedom to Eastern Europe, Central America, and Africa. The three of them would work closely together to bring greater liberation to various parts of the world.

The four pillars of Reagan's economic policy were to reduce government spending, reduce the rates of income taxes and capital gains taxes, reduce government regulation, and control the money supply to reduce inflation. His policies—along with supply-side economics, the Laffer Curve, and trickle-down economics—would become known as Reaganomics.

On August 13, 1981, President Reagan signed sweeping tax cuts into law. Marginal tax rates for individuals were lowered from 70 percent to 28 percent. Starting in 1981 Reagan presided over the rebuilding of a military that was dramatically reduced by President Carter and the Democrats in Congress.

The Great Communicator

On November 6, 1984, Reagan was re-elected in a landslide victory over Walter Mondale and Geraldine Ferraro. The president would ask the voters, "Are you better off today than you were four years ago?" The Reagan-Bush ticket would win every state except Mondale's home state of Minnesota.

Unable to explain his popularity, the left gave Reagan the nickname, "the Great Communicator." He responded to the nickname in his farewell speech.

> I never thought it was my style of the words I used that made a difference: It was the content. I wasn't a great communicator, but I communicated great things, and they didn't spring full bloom from my brow, they came from the heart of a great nation—from our experience, our wisdom, and our belief in the principles that have guided us for two centuries.

In August 1980, in the shipyards of Gdansk, Poland, a labor union began to protest the Communist government. The Polish Communist government tried to break up the movement by instituting martial law in 1981.

Ronald Wilson Reagan

Solidarity, with its leader, Lech Walesa, grew to over 10 million members and, with the financial and moral support of the Reagan administration, freed Poland. In December 1990 Walesa was elected Poland's president. Walesa gave Reagan due credit, saying, "When talking about Ronald Reagan, I have to be personal. We in Poland took him so personally. Why? Because we owe him our liberty. This can't be said often enough by people who lived under oppression for half a century, until communism fell in 1989. Poles fought for their freedom for so many years that they hold in special esteem those who backed them in their struggle. Support was a test of friendship. President Reagan was such a friend. His policy of aiding democratic movements in Central and Eastern Europe in the dark days of the Cold War meant a lot to us."

As president, Ronald Reagan was committed to ridding the world of nuclear weapons. He sought discussions with successive Soviet leaders, but, as Reagan put it at the time, "They keep dying on me." Finally, in Mikhail Gorbachev, Reagan found a Soviet

The Great Communicator

leader with whom he could discuss the issue of nuclear weapons. At a summit in Geneva in 1985, he established a rapport with Gorbachev and staked out his positions. Then, in 1986, at a summit in Reykjavik, Iceland, the two leaders came within reach of an agreement to make substantial reductions in their respective nuclear arsenals. However, Gorbachev insisted that in exchange, the United States drop its Strategic Defense Initiative (SDI). As a good negotiator, Reagan knew when it was time to walk away from the table, and, despite his bitter disappointment, he did so.

Reagan's persistence and commitment to principle were rewarded in 1987, when he and Gorbachev signed an agreement to eliminate an entire class of nuclear weapons, the so-called Intermediate Nuclear Forces (INF) treaty. As Reagan famously told Gorbachev at the time, the American president would, relying on a Russian maxim, "trust, but verify," referring to the treaty's verification provisions.

In one of his most famous speeches, both

Ronald Wilson Reagan

for its boldness and its call to action, President Reagan challenged Soviet Communist Party General Secretary Mikhail Gorbachev in a speech at the Brandenburg Gate of the Berlin Wall. The speech was given on June 12, 1987, in front of the dark symbol of the repression of Communism. Built in 1961 to keep East Germans from leaving the Communist country, it became the centerpiece of the Soviet Iron Curtain.

Reagan said to a crowd of Germans,

> We welcome change and openness; for we believe that freedom and security go together, that the advance of human liberty can only strengthen the cause of world peace. There is one sign the Soviets can make that would be unmistakable, that would advance dramatically the cause of freedom and peace. General Secretary Gorbachev, if you seek peace, if you seek prosperity for the Soviet Union and Eastern Europe, if you seek liberalization, come here to this gate. Mr. Gorbachev, open this gate. Mr. Gorbachev, tear down this wall!

The Great Communicator

Late in his speech, Reagan ad-libbed,

> As I looked out a moment ago from the Reichstag, that embodiment of German unity, I noticed words crudely spray-painted upon the wall, perhaps by a young Berliner. "This wall will fall. Beliefs become reality." Yes, across Europe, this wall will fall. For it cannot withstand faith; it cannot withstand truth. The wall cannot withstand freedom.

Two and a half years later, as Ronald Reagan enjoyed his retirement in Los Angeles, on November 9, 1989, the Berlin Wall fell. He would live to see democracy and freedom rise in Czechoslovakia (1989), Romania (1989), Hungary (1989), Poland (1989), East Germany (1989), and Nicaragua (1990). Even China would see pro-democracy protests at Tiananmen Square in April 1989.

On January 11, 1989, the president delivered his farewell address. He sat at his Oval Office desk with his broad shoulders and soft features and spoke to the nation he loved—a nation that also grew to love him for his courageous and compassionate leadership.

Ronald Wilson Reagan

Because we're a great nation, our challenges seem complex. It will always be this way. But as long as we remember our first principles and believe in ourselves, the future will always be ours. And something else we learned: Once you begin a great movement, there's no telling where it will end. We meant to change a nation, and instead, we changed a world.

I have spoken of the shining city all my political life, but I don't know if I ever quite communicated what I saw when I said it. But in my mind it was a tall proud city built on rocks stronger than oceans, wind-swept, God-blessed, and teeming with people of all kinds living in harmony and peace, a city with free ports that hummed with commerce and creativity, and if there had to be city walls, the walls had doors and the doors were open to anyone with the will and the heart to get here. That's how I saw it, and see it still.

And how stands the city on this winter night? More prosperous, more secure, and happier than it was eight years ago. But more than that; after two hundred years, two centuries, she still stands strong and true on that granite ridge, and her glow

The Great Communicator

has held steady no matter what storm. And she's still a beacon, still a magnet for all who must have freedom, for all the pilgrims from all the lost places who are hurtling through the darkness, toward home.

We've done our part. And as I walk off into the city streets, a final word to the men and women of the Reagan Revolution, the men and women across America who for eight years did the work that brought America back. My friends: We did it. We weren't just marking time. We made a difference. We made the city stronger. We made the city freer, and we left her in good hands. All in all, not bad, not bad at all. And so, good-bye, God bless you, and God bless the United States of America.

The numbers and facts would become stubborn things, as Reagan would say. In the eight years he was president, over 20 million new jobs were created, there were ninety-two months of economic growth without a recession (the second-longest period of growth in U.S. history), and massive cuts in tax rates yielded a near doubling of federal tax reve-

Ronald Wilson Reagan

nues from $517 billion in 1980 to $1 trillion in 1990. The gross domestic product grew by nearly 36 percent, and the U.S. economy grew by more than a third.

While opening the Reagan Presidential Library in Simi Valley, California, in 1991, the former president declared,

> I know in my heart that man is good, that what is right will always eventually triumph, and there is purpose and worth to each and every life.

On November 5, 1994, President Reagan would publicly communicate with his beloved fellow citizens one more time, this time to announce he had Alzheimer's disease. He would do so in the form of a letter of gratitude, concluding as follows:

> In closing let me thank you, the American people, for giving me the great honor of allowing me to serve as your President. When the Lord calls me home, whenever that may be, I will leave with the greatest love for this country of ours and eternal optimism for its future. I now begin the journey that will lead me into the sunset

The Great Communicator

> of my life. I know that for America there will always be a bright new dawn ahead. Thank you, my friends. May God always bless you.

On the morning of June 5, 2004, the former president's health had significantly deteriorated, following ten years of insidious disease. According to Reagan's daughter, Patti Davis, "At the last moment, when his breathing told us this was it, he opened his eyes and looked straight at my mother. Eyes that hadn't opened for days did, and they weren't chalky or vague. They were clear and blue and full of love. If a death can be lovely, his was." Nancy Reagan told him that the moment was "the greatest gift you could have given me." President Reagan died of pneumonia at his home at 1:09 pm. At his side were his wife and two of his children, Ron and Patti. Daughter Maureen had preceded him in death at age sixty, in 2001, of melanoma. His eldest son, Michael, was with his father the day before.

President George W. Bush said in a statement at the knowledge of his passing:

Ronald Wilson Reagan

"Ronald Reagan won America's respect with his greatness, and won its love with his goodness. He had the confidence that comes with conviction, the strength that comes with character, the grace that comes with humility, and the humor that comes with wisdom. He leaves behind a nation he restored and a world he helped save."

Ronald Reagan summed up his philosophy on life in his own words:

> Life is one grand, sweet song, so start the music.

Bibliography

D'Souza, Dinesh. *Ronald Reagan: How an Ordinary Man Became an Extraordinary Leader*. New York: Free Press, 1997.

Edwards, Anne. *Early Reagan: The Rise to Power*. New York: William Morrow and Company, 1987.

Eliot, Marc. *Reagan: The Hollywood Years*. New York: Rebel Road, 2008.

Goldman, Peter, et al. *The Quest for the Presidency 1984*. Toronto: Bantam Books, 1985.

Meese, Edwin, III. *With Reagan: The Inside Story*. Washington, DC: Regnery Gateway, 1992.

Noonan, Peggy. *What I Saw of the Revolution*. New York: Random House, 1990.

———. *When Character Was King*. New York: Penguin Group, 2001.

Reagan, Ronald. *An American Life: The Autobiography of Ronald Reagan*. New York: Simon and Schuster, 1990.

———. *Reagan: A Life In Letters*. New York: Simon & Schuster, 2003.

———, with Richard G. Hubler. *Ronald Reagan's Own Story: Where's the Rest of Me?* New York: Karz-Segil Publishers, 1966.

Von Damm, Helene. *At Reagan's Side: 20 Years in the Political Mainstream*. New York: Doubleday, 1989.

White, F. Clifton, and William J. Gill. *Why Reagan Won: The Conservative Movement 1964–1981*. Chicago: Regnery Gateway, 1981.

About Greg Rothman

Greg Rothman is President/CEO of RSR REALTORS in Harrisburg, Pennsylvania. He received his Bachelor's of Science in Political Science from the University of Massachusetts at Amherst and a Master's of Science in Real Estate from Johns Hopkins University. He is a veteran of the U.S. Marine Corps and was appointed by President George W. Bush to the National Veterans Business Development Corporation. He has advised and worked for numerous political campaigns. An avid reader with a passion for studying lives of great business and political leaders, he is the author of *The 7 Golden Rules of Milton Hershey* and *Ronald Reagan: The Great Communicator*.

Author Greg Rothman with Ronald Reagan in May 1991 in the former president's Los Angeles, California, office.

The *Life-Changing Classics* and *Laws of Leadership* series bring you timeless wisdom in compact, affordable editions! Available now at www.TremendousLifeBooks.com!

Greg Rothman, *Ronald Wilson Reagan*

Charlie "Tremendous" Jones, *The Price of Leadership*

Charles Schwab, *Succeeding With What You Have*

Andrew Carnegie, *Advantages of Poverty*

Russell Conwell, *Acres of Diamonds*

John Wanamaker, *Maxims of Life and Business With Selected Prayers*

Charlie "Tremendous" Jones, *Books Are Tremendous*

William W. Woodbridge, *"Bradford, You're Fired!"*

James Allen, *As a Man Thinketh*

R.A. Laidlaw, *The Reason Why*

Elbert Hubbard, *A Message to Garcia*

Booker T. Washington, *Character Building*

William W. Woodbridge, *That Something*

Orison Swett Marden, *Self-Improvement Through Public Speaking*

Greg Rothman, *The 7 Golden Rules of Milton Hershey*

Henry Drummond, *The Greatest Thing in the World*

William George Jordan, *The Kingship of Self-Control*

George S. Patton, *The Wit and Wisdom of General George S. Patton*

Charles Spurgeon, *My Conversion*

Wallace D. Wattles, *The Science of Getting Rich*

Albert E.N. Gray, *The New Common Denominator of Success*

Abraham Lincoln, *The Lincoln Ideals*

Share the warmth, wisdom and humor of beloved speaker and author Charlie "Tremendous" Jones!

- Books
- CDs
- DVDs

...And much more at Charlie's home on the web, www.TremendousLifeBooks.com